MW00629958

THE ART OF
DRAWING

HOW TO DRAW TATTOOS

A HELPFUL MANUAL FOR
ARTISTS AND DESIGNERS

STEP BY STEP

HAND DRAWN
UNIQUE **40** DESIGNS
BEST QUALITY

EDITIONS
Vault

VAULT EDITIONS

INTRODUCTION

Tattoos have transcended mere body art to become powerful forms of self-expression, telling unique stories etched into the canvas of one's skin. For those captivated by the world of tattoos, whether you're a budding artist or a design enthusiast, *How to Draw Tattoos* is your gateway to unlocking the secrets of this captivating craft. This book is designed with beginners in mind, offering a progressive learning system that empowers even those with no prior drawing experience to embark on a creative journey like no other.

In this comprehensive guide, we dive deep into the captivating world of traditional tattoo styles. You'll discover the rich symbolism and timeless allure of tattoo designs such as eagles, swallows, skulls, gorillas, owls, grim reapers, sacred hearts, panthers, tigers, koi fish, dragons, and so much more. Our step-by-step approach ensures that you learn to draw these iconic designs and understand the cultural and historical significance behind each design featured.

So, whether you dream of becoming a tattoo artist, want to design your own tattoos, or wish to appreciate this ancient art form on a deeper level, *How to Draw Tattoos* is your ideal companion. Embark on this creative adventure, and let your passion for traditional tattoo styles come to life. Unleash your inner artist and turn your imagination into beautiful, meaningful, and timeless designs that transcend the boundaries of art and skin.

TABLE ◇OF◇ CONTENTS

DOWNLOAD YOUR FILES

Downloading your files is simple. To access your digital files, please go to the last page of this book and follow the instructions.

For technical assistance, please email:
info@vaulteditions.com

Copyright

Bibliographical Note

This book is a new work created by Vault Editions Ltd.

ISBN: 978-1-922966-23-0

VAULT EDITIONS

EAGLE ONE

An eagle tattoo symbolises freedom and vision. It can also represent courage, patriotism, or a connection to nature. Personal interpretations may vary.

01

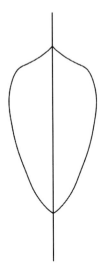

02

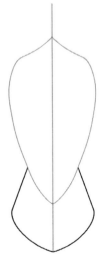

03

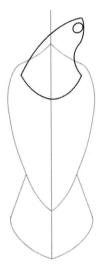

04

05

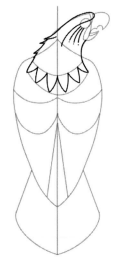

06

07

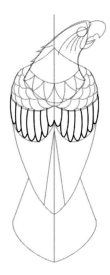

08

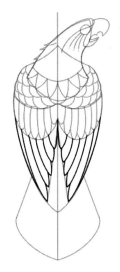

09

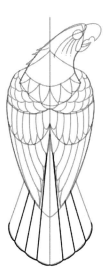

10

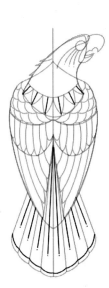

11

12

HOW TO DRAW TATTOOS

EAGLE TWO

HOW TO DRAW TATTOOS

An eagle tattoo can also symbolise power
and majesty. It can represent inspiration,
leadership, or a connection to the skies.
Personal meanings may vary.

01

02

03

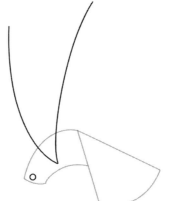

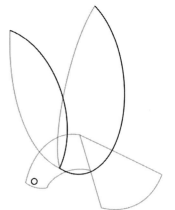

04

05

06

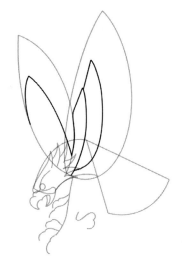

07

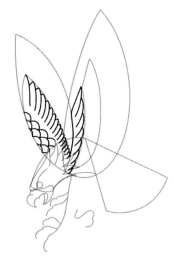

08

09

10

11

GORILLA ONE

A gorilla tattoo symbolises power and strength. Personal interpretations may vary.

01

02

03

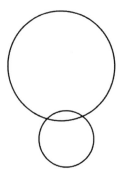

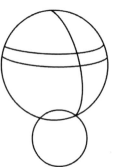

04

05

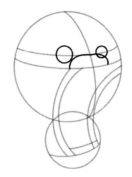

06

07

08

09

10

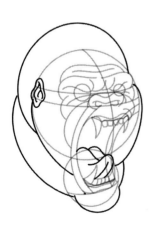

11

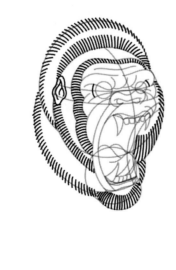

12

GORILLA TWO

A gorilla tattoo can also symbolise courage, family, or a connection to the animal kingdom. Personal interpretations may vary.

01

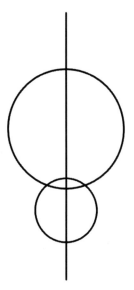

02

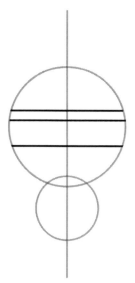

03

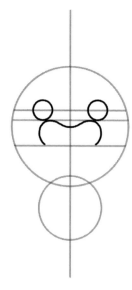

04

05

06

07

08

09

10

11

12

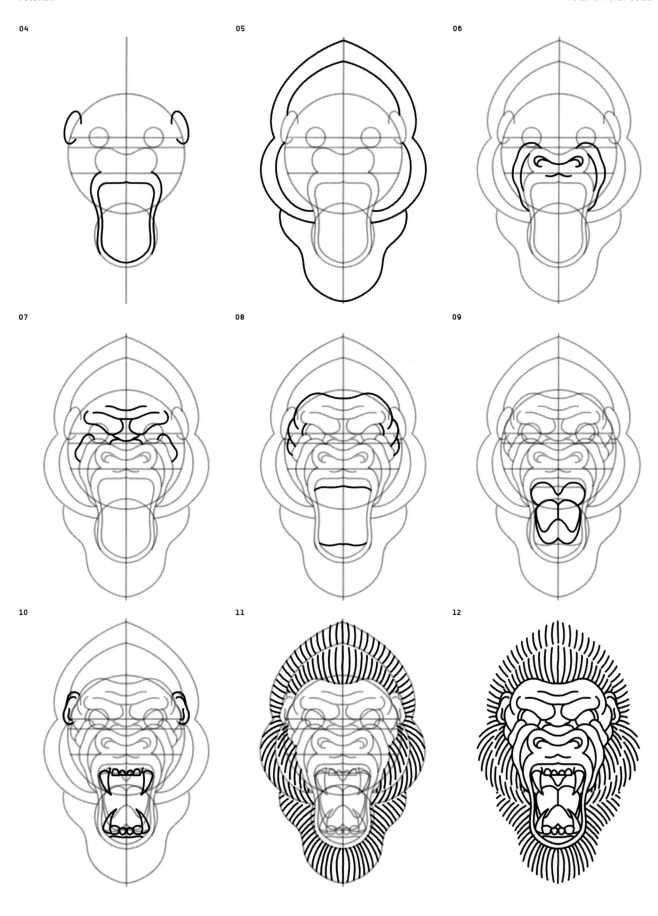

HOW TO DRAW TATTOOS

HOW TO DRAW TATTOOS

HANYA MASK

A Hannya mask tattoo symbolises duality, anger, and transformation. It can represent inner struggles, protection, or a connection to Japanese folklore. Interpretations vary.

01

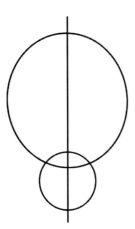

02

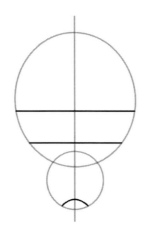

03

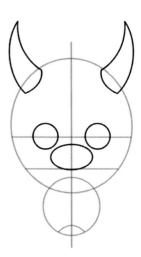

04
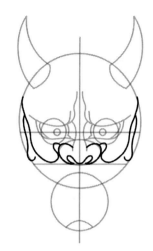

05
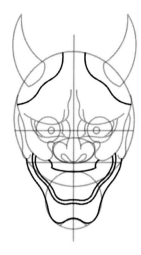

06

07

08
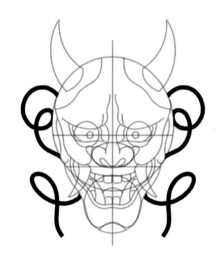

09

10
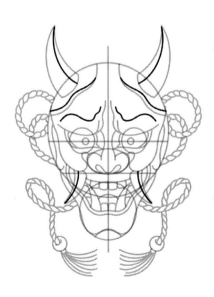

11

HOW TO DRAW TATTOOS

ANCHOR

An anchor tattoo symbolises stability and strength. It can also represent a connection to the sea, a love for maritime life, or a reminder of a significant life event. It may have various personal meanings for individuals.

01

02

03

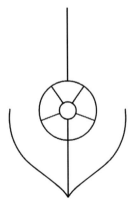

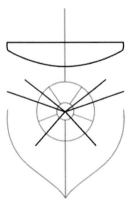

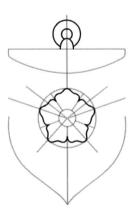

04

05

06

07

08

09

10

HOW TO DRAW TATTOOS

BAT

A bat tattoo can symbolise protection, good luck, and prosperity. It can also represent mystery, night, and rebirth. It can also signify a connection to the supernatural. Interpretations can vary.

01

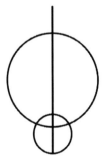

02

03

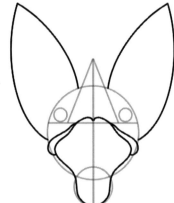

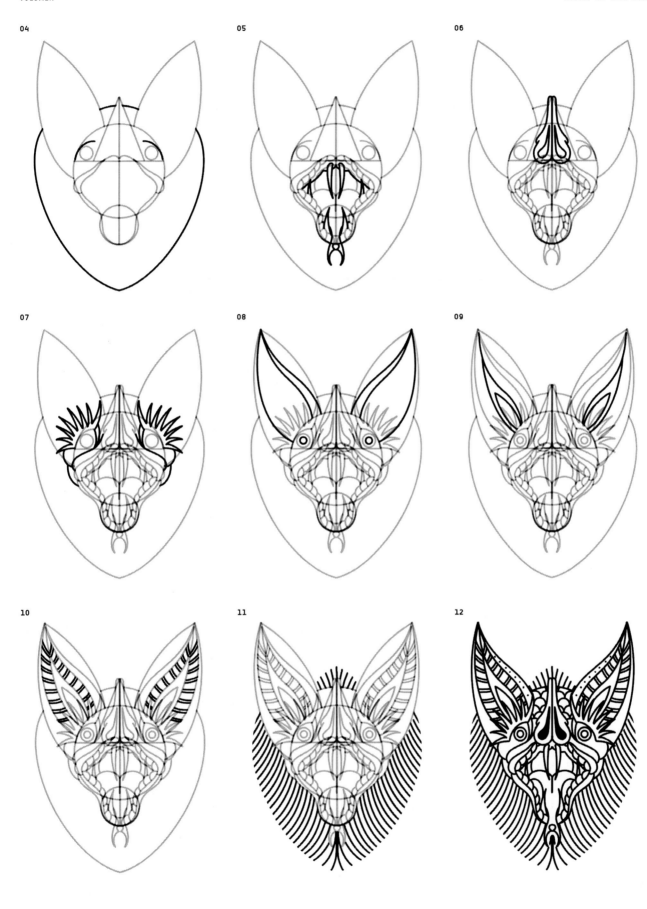

BEAR

A bear tattoo symbolises courage and strength. It can also represent protection, leadership, or a spiritual connection. Meanings may differ.

01

02

03

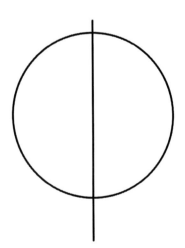

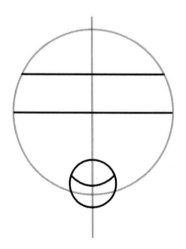

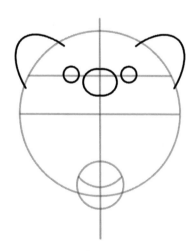

04

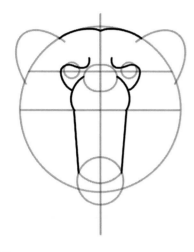

05

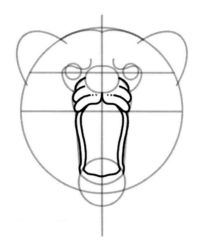

06

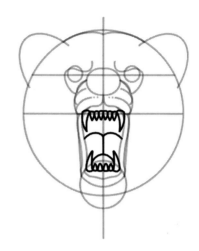

07

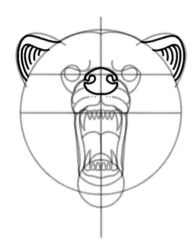

08

09

HOW TO DRAW TATTOOS

10

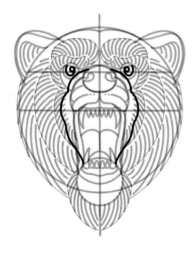

11

BUTTERFLY LADY

A butterfly lady tattoo can symbolise transformation and beauty. It may represent femininity, freedom, or a love for nature. Individual interpretations can vary widely.

01

02

03

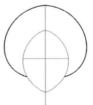

04

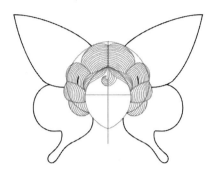

05

06

07

08

09

10

11

12

SWALLOW

A swallow tattoo symbolises hope, love, and loyalty. It can also signify a return home or safe passage. Personal meanings may differ from person to person.

01

02

03

04

05

06

07

08

09

HOW TO DRAW TATTOOS

SWALLOW TWO

A swallow tattoo can also symbolise freedom and travel. It often represents overcoming challenges and finding one's way back to a safe haven. Interpretations may vary.

01

02

03

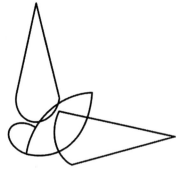

04

05

06

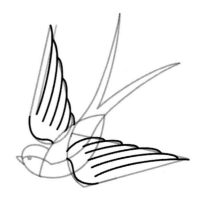

07

08

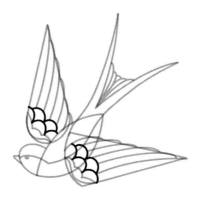

09

10

BUTTERFLY

A butterfly tattoo symbolises transformation and beauty. It can also signify personal growth, freedom, or a connection to nature. Individual interpretations may differ widely.

01   02   03

04

05

06

07

08

09

10

11

12

COBRA SNAKE

A cobra snake tattoo symbolises power and danger. It can represent protection, transformation, or a connection to the mystical. Personal meanings may vary.

01   02   03

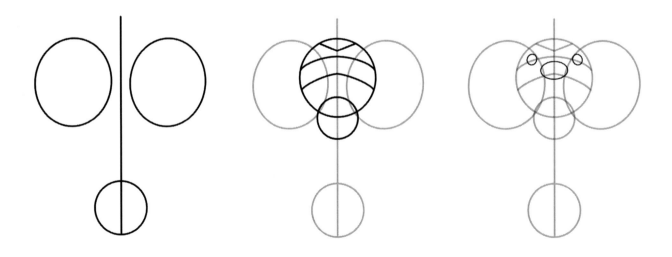

04

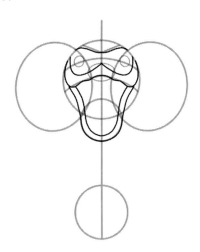

05

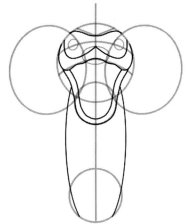

06

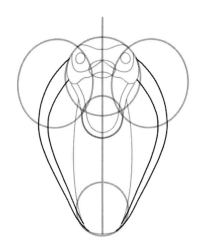

07

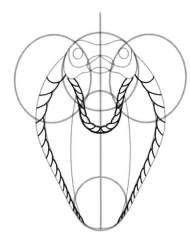

08

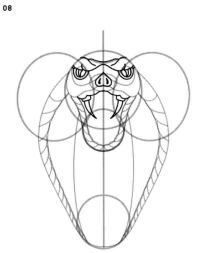

09

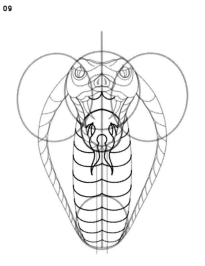

10

11

SNAKE HEAD

A snake tattoo symbolizes transformation, rebirth, and adaptability. It can represent healing, danger, or a connection to the primal and mysterious. Personal interpretations may differ widely.

01

02

03

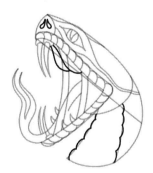
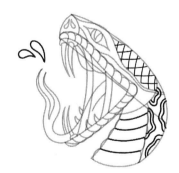

HOW TO DRAW TATTOOS

CRYING HEART

A crying heart tattoo symbolizes deep emotional pain or loss. It can also represent love, sorrow, or a difficult life experience. Interpretations may differ based on personal emotions and experiences.

01

02

03

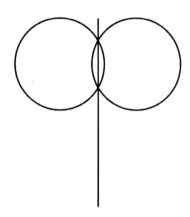

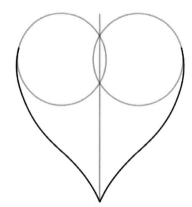

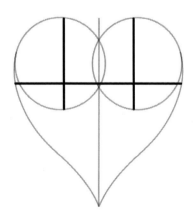

04

05

06

07

08

09

10

11

DRAGON

A dragon tattoo symbolises strength and
wisdom. It can represent protection,
prosperity, or a connection to mythology.
Personal meanings can vary widely.

HOW TO DRAW TATTOOS

01

02

03

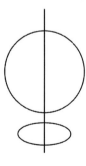

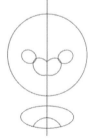

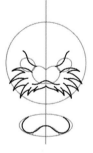

04

05

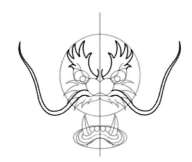

06

07

08

09

10

EYE OF THE STORM

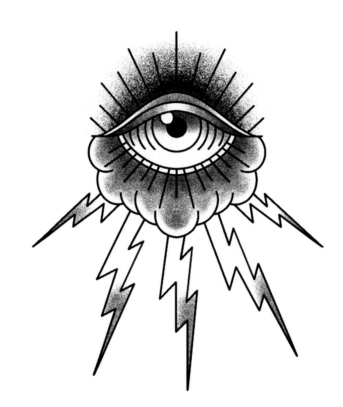

An eye of the storm tattoo symbolises calm in chaos and resilience. It can represent inner peace, weathering challenges, or a metaphor for staying strong during turbulent times. Interpretations can vary.

01   02   03

  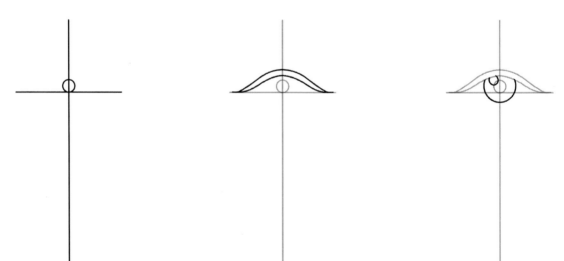

04
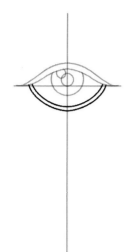

05
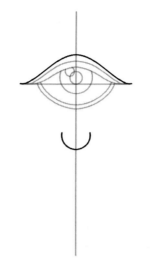

06
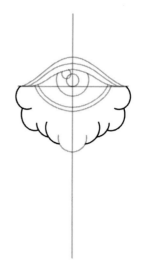

07

08

09

10

11

12

HOW TO DRAW TATTOOS

GYPSY LADY

A gypsy lady tattoo can symbolise mystery and independence. It often represents a free spirit, wanderlust, or a connection to the Romani culture. Meanings may differ.

01

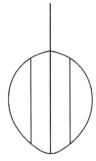

02

03

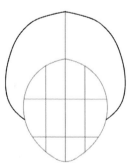

04
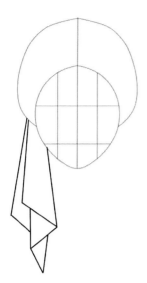

05
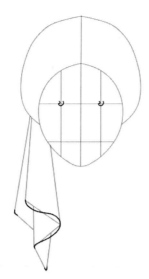

06
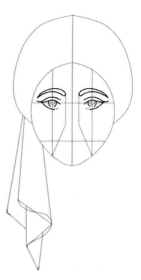

07

08

09

10

11

12

SACRED HEART

A Sacred Heart tattoo symbolises love, devotion, and spirituality. It can represent faith, compassion, or a deep connection to one's beliefs. Interpretations may differ.

01

02

03

04

05

06

07

08

09

10

KOI FISH

A Koi fish tattoo symbolises perseverance, determination, and transformation. It often represents overcoming adversity, ambition, or a connection to Asian culture. Personal meanings may vary.

01

02

03

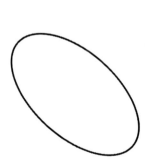

04

05

06

07

08

09

10

11

12

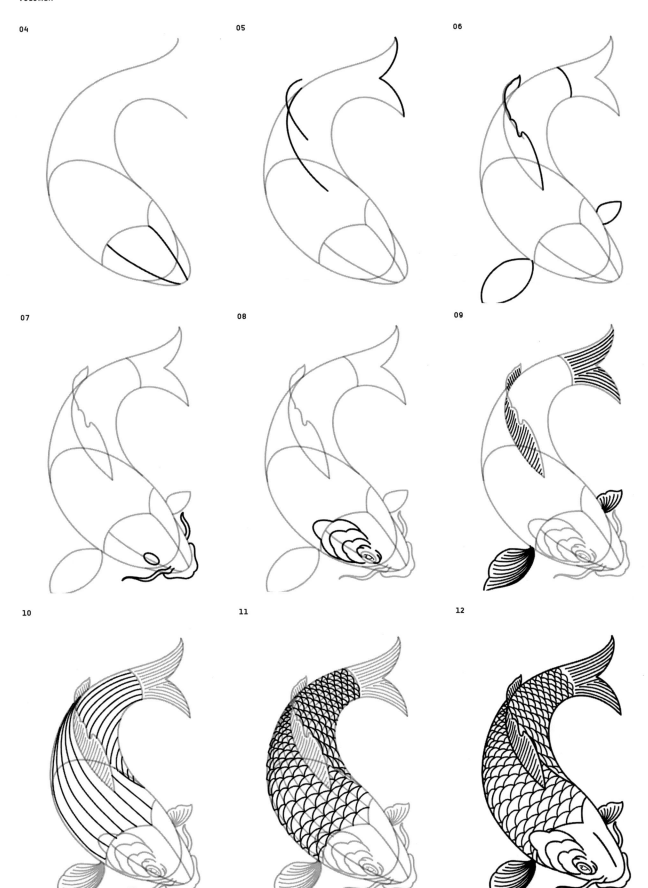

MOTH

A moth tattoo symbolises determination and transformation. It can represent vulnerability, or a fascination with the night. Personal meanings may vary.

01

02

03

04

05

06

07

08

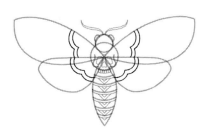

09

10

11

12

OWL ONE

HOW TO DRAW TATTOOS

An owl tattoo symbolises wisdom, intuition, and mystery. It may represent knowledge, protection, or a connection to the nocturnal world. Interpretations can vary widely.

01

02

03

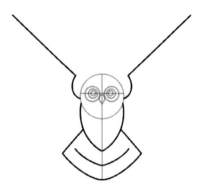

04

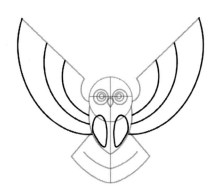

05

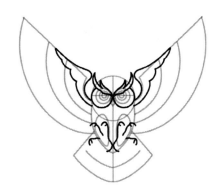

06

07

08

09

10

HOW TO DRAW TATTOOS

OWL TWO

An owl tattoo can also symbolise insight, change, and vision. It often represents a deep connection to nature, spirituality, or the ability to see beyond the surface. Personal meanings may differ.

01

02

03

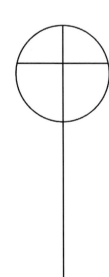

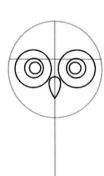

04

05

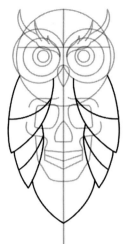

06

07

08

09

10

PANTHER ONE

A panther tattoo symbolises courage, strength, and ferocity. It can represent independence, stealth, or a connection to primal instincts. Personal interpretations may vary widely.

01

02

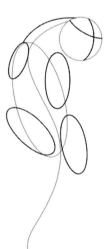

03

04

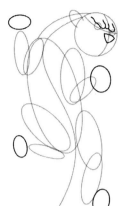

05

06

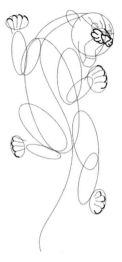

07

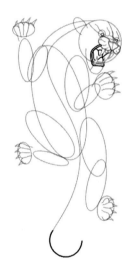

08

09

10

HOW TO DRAW TATTOOS

HOW TO DRAW TATTOOS

PANTHER TWO

A panther and dagger tattoo symbolises courage, danger, and protection. It can represent a fearless spirit, the readiness to confront threats, or a blend of strength and resilience. Personal meanings may vary.

01

02

03

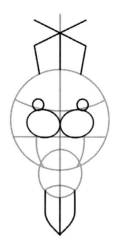

04

05
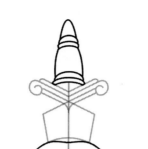

06

07
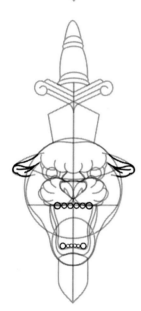

08
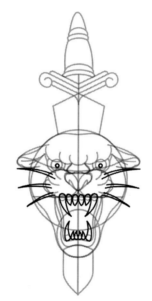

09

10

PANTHER THREE

A panther tattoo can also symbolise resilience, adaptability, and leadership. It often represents a fierce spirit and the ability to overcome challenges. Personal interpretations can vary.

01

02

03

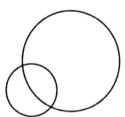

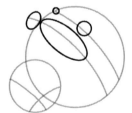

04

05

06

07

08

09

10

PIG

A pig tattoo can symbolise luck, protection, and sea-faring. In western culture they are often associated with sailors and signify safety at sea, good fortune, and a love for adventure. Interpretations can vary.

01

02

03

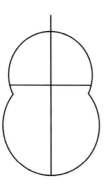

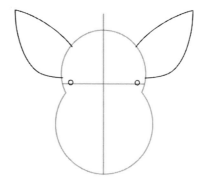

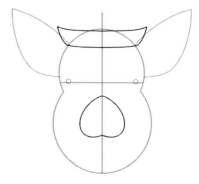

04

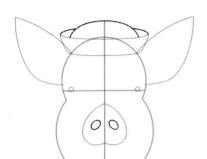

05

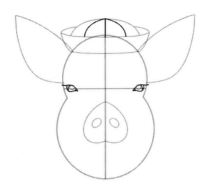

06

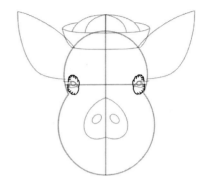

07

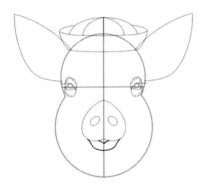

08

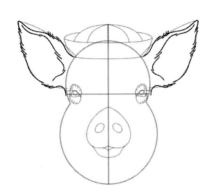

09

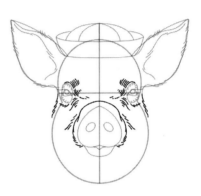

HOW TO DRAW TATTOOS

10

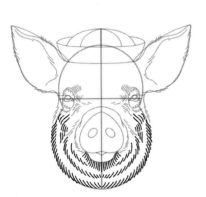

11

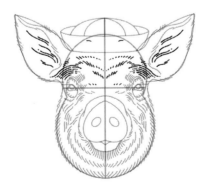

12

ROOSTER

A rooster tattoo can symbolise luck, protection, and balance. They are often associated with sailors and signify safety at sea, prosperity, and a harmonious journey. Personal meanings may vary widely.

01

02

03

04
05
06

07
08
09

10
11

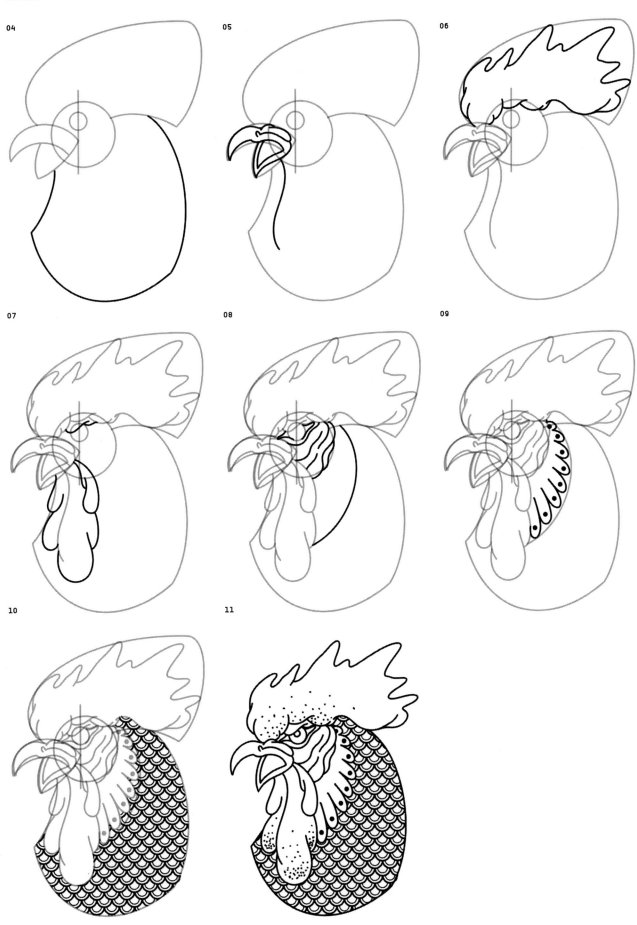

REAPER

A reaper tattoo symbolises mortality and the inevitability of death. It can represent a reminder of life's impermanence, transformation, or a fascination with the macabre. Interpretations may differ.

01

02

03

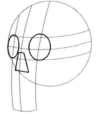

04

05

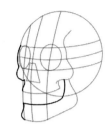

06

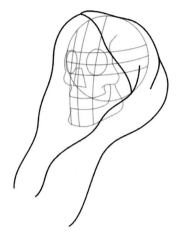

07

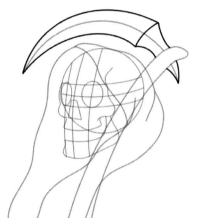

08

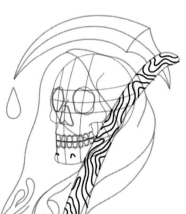

09

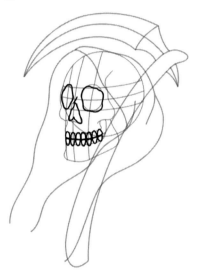

10

11

12

ROSE

A rose tattoo symbolises love, beauty, and passion. It can represent romance, remembrance, or a connection to emotions. Personal meanings may vary widely.

01

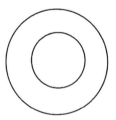

02

03

04

05

06

07

08

09

10

11

ROSE & SKULL

A rose and skull tattoo symbolises the duality of life and death. It often represents the beauty in impermanence, remembrance, or the merging of contrasting elements. Interpretations can vary widely.

01

02

03

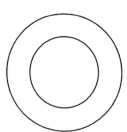

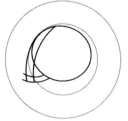

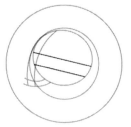

04

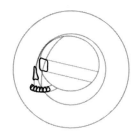

05

06

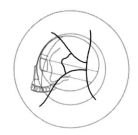

07

08

09

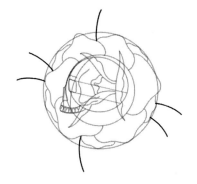

10

11

SCORPION

A scorpion tattoo is a symbol of power, protection, and transformation. It can represent resilience, a connection to the zodiac, or a fearless spirit. Interpretations may differ.

01

02

03

04

05

06

07

08

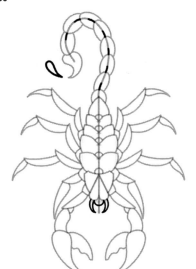

09

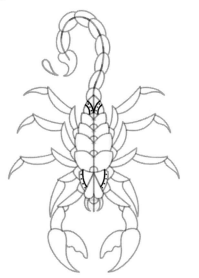

10

HOW TO DRAW TATTOOS

HOW TO DRAW TATTOOS

SHARK

A shark tattoo symbolises power, strength, and determination. It can represent fearlessness, adaptability, or a fascination with the ocean. Personal meanings may vary.

01

02

03

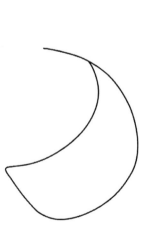

04

05

06

HOW TO DRAW TATTOOS

SHIP

HOW TO DRAW TATTOOS

A ship tattoo symbolises a journey, adventure, and exploration. It can represent the pursuit of dreams, freedom, or a connection to maritime life. Personal interpretations may differ widely.

01

02

03

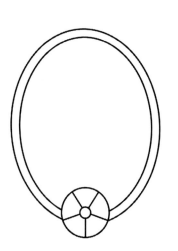

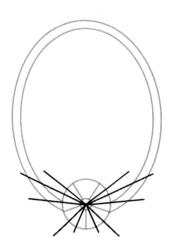

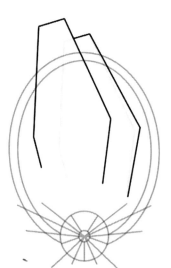

04

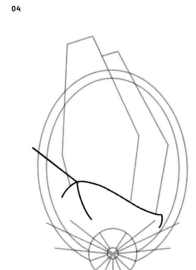

05

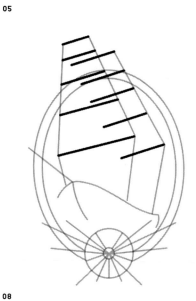

06

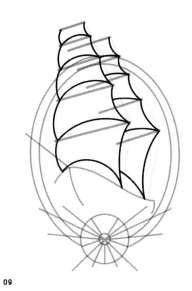

07

08

09

10

11

HOW TO DRAW TATTOOS

SKULL

A skull tattoo symbolises mortality, life's fragility, and the balance between life and death. It can represent remembrance, rebellion, or a fascination with the macabre. Personal meanings may vary.

01

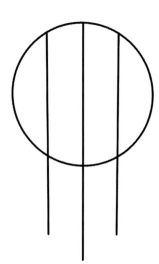

02

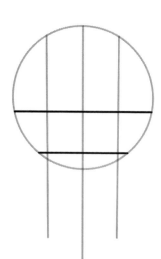

03

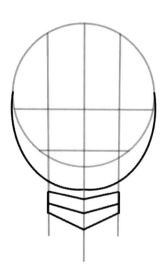

04

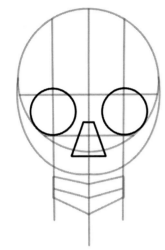

05

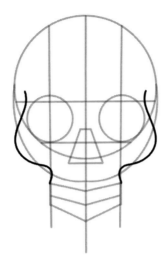

06

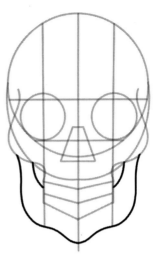

07

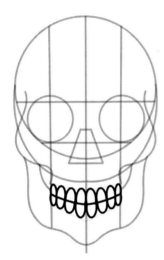

08

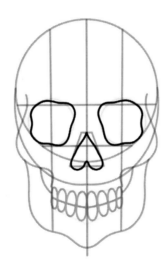

09

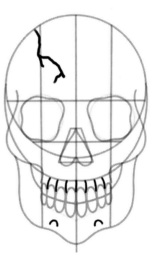

HOW TO DRAW TATTOOS

10

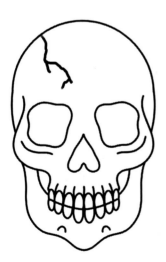

SPIDER

A spider tattoo symbolises creativity, patience, and intrigue. It can represent weaving one's destiny, complexity, or a connection to the mysterious and crafty. Personal meanings may vary.

01   02   03

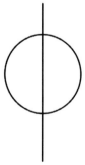

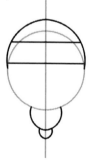

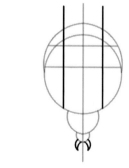

04

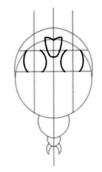

05

06

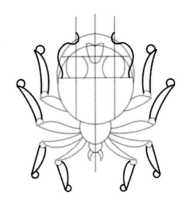

07

08

09

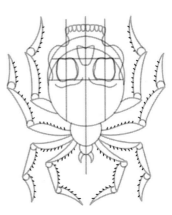

10

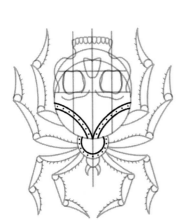

11

12

TIGER

A tiger tattoo symbolises strength, power, and bravery. It can represent protection, courage, or a connection to the wild and untamed. Personal interpretations may differ.

01

02

03

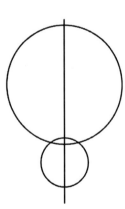

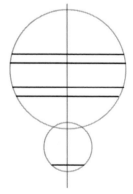

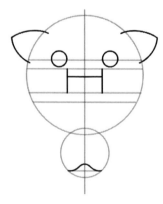

04

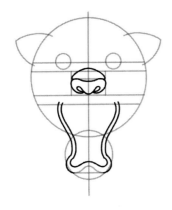

05

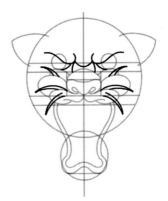

06

07

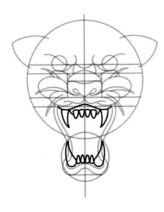

08

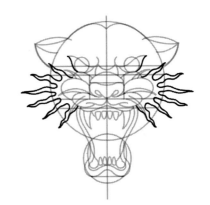

09

10

11

12

TRUST NO ONE

A "Trust No One" tattoo symbolises caution, self-reliance, and skepticism. It can represent a guarded attitude, wariness, or a reminder to prioritize personal safety. Interpretations may vary in different cultures.

01

02

03

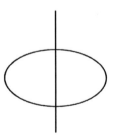

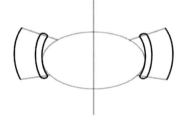

04

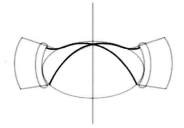

05

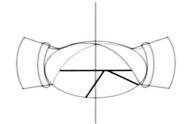

06

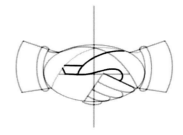

07

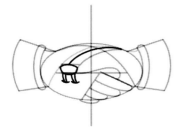

08

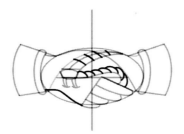

09

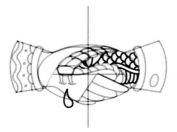

10

UMBRELLA

HOW TO DRAW TATTOOS

An umbrella tattoo symbolises protection, shelter, and adaptability. It can represent security, resilience, or a connection to the rain and weather. Personal meanings may differ.

01

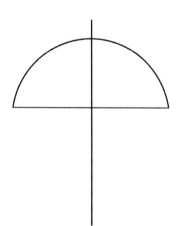

02

03

04

05

06

07

08

09

10

11

WOLF

HOW TO DRAW TATTOOS

A wolf tattoo symbolises freedom, instinct, and resilience. It can represent independence, loyalty, or a connection to the untamed wilderness. Interpretations may vary.

01

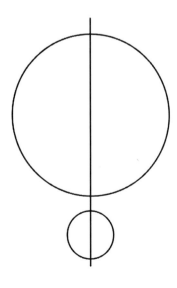

02

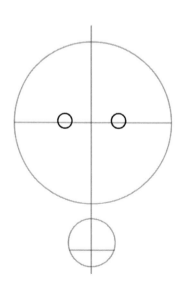

03

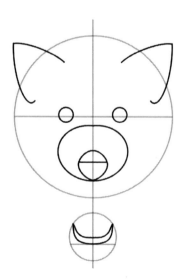

04

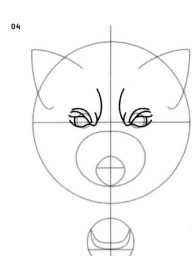

05

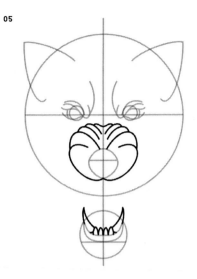

06

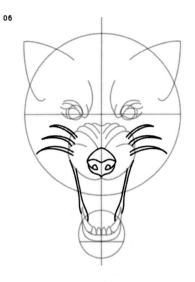

07

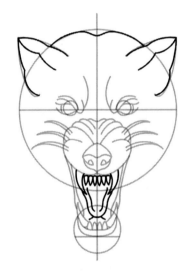

08

09

10

HOW TO DRAW TATTOOS

PRACTICE MAKES PERFECT
HOW TO DRAW TATTOOS
PRACTICE MAKES PERFECT

Vault Editions Ltd

LEARN MORE

VAULTEDITIONS.COM

PRACTICE MAKES PERFECT
T R D   M R K

HOW TO DRAW
TATTOOS

PRACTICE MAKES PERFECT
T R D   M R K

Vault Editions Ltd

CURATION AND RESTORATION SERVICES

LEARN MORE

VAULTEDITIONS.COM

PRACTICE MAKES PERFECT
T R D   M R K

HOW TO DRAW
TATTOOS

PRACTICE MAKES PERFECT
T R D   M R K

Vault Editions Ltd

CURATION AND RESTORATION SERVICES

LEARN MORE

VAULTEDITIONS.COM

PRACTICE
MAKES
PERFECT
T R D
M R K

HOW TO DRAW
TATTOOS

Vault Editions Ltd

CURATION AND RESTORATION SERVICES

LEARN MORE

VAULTEDITIONS.COM

PRACTICE MAKES PERFECT
T R D   M R K

HOW TO DRAW
TATTOOS

PRACTICE MAKES PERFECT
T R D   M R K

Vault Editions Ltd

CORATION AND RESTORATION SERVICES

HOW TO DRAW
TATTOOS

PRACTICE
MAKES
PERFECT
TRD MRK

PRACTICE
MAKES
PERFECT
TRD MRK

HOW TO DRAW TATTOOS

Vault Editions Ltd

CURATION AND RESTORATION SERVICES

LEARN MORE

VAULTEDITIONS.COM

PRACTICE
T R D | MAKES | M R K
PERFECT

HOW TO DRAW
TATTOOS

PRACTICE
T R D | MAKES | M R K
PERFECT

Vault Editions Ltd

CURATION AND RESTORATION SERVICES

LEARN MORE

VAULTEDITIONS.COM

PRACTICE
T R D   MAKES   M R K
PERFECT

HOW TO DRAW
TATTOOS

PRACTICE
T R D   MAKES   M R K
PERFECT

HOW TO DRAW TATTOOS

Vault Editions Ltd

LEARN MORE

VAULTEDITIONS.COM

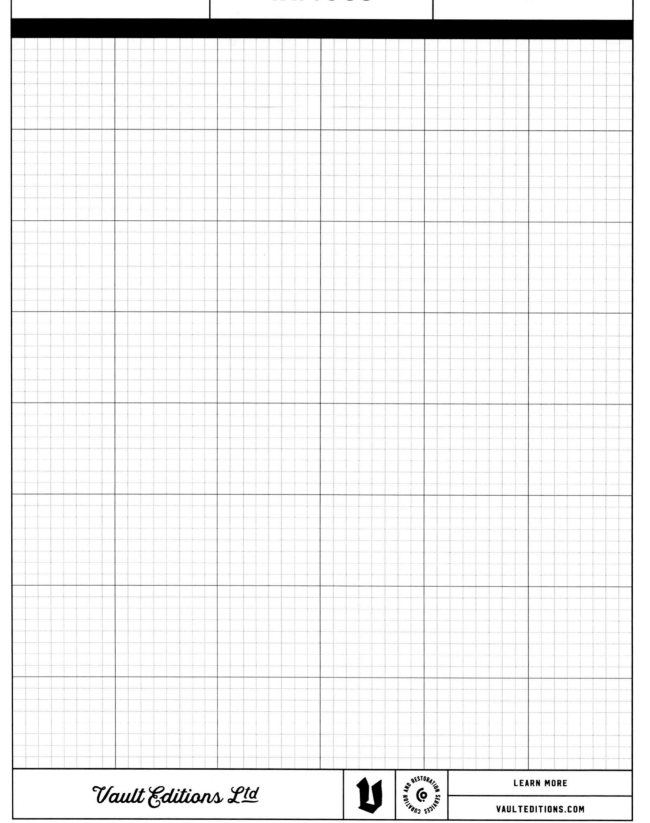

PRACTICE MAKES PERFECT — TRD MRK

HOW TO DRAW
TATTOOS

PRACTICE MAKES PERFECT — TRD MRK

Vault Editions Ltd

CURATION AND RESTORATION SERVICES

LEARN MORE

VAULTEDITIONS.COM

PRACTICE MAKES PERFECT
T R D   M R K

HOW TO DRAW
TATTOOS

PRACTICE MAKES PERFECT
T R D   M R K

Vault Editions Ltd

CURATION AND RESTORATION SERVICES

LEARN MORE

VAULTEDITIONS.COM

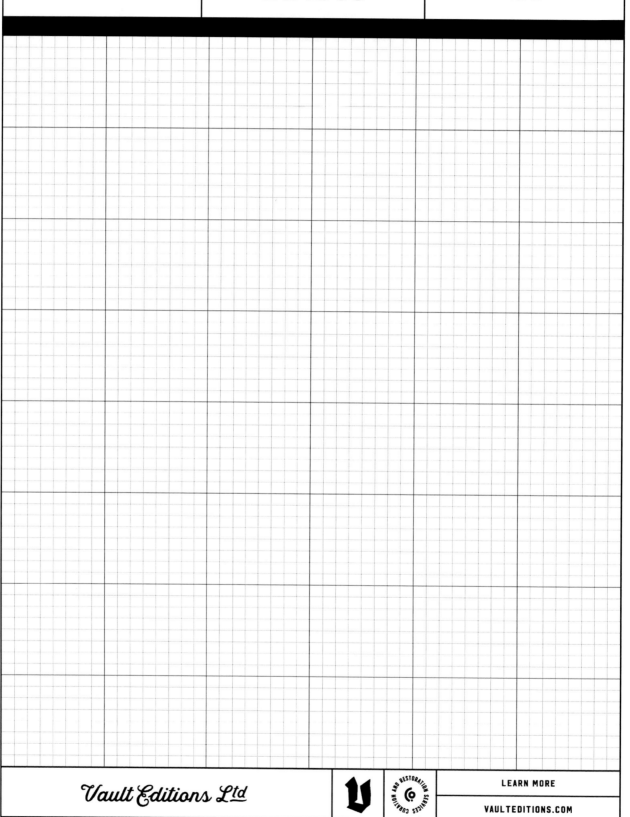

PRACTICE MAKES PERFECT
T R D   M R K

HOW TO DRAW
TATTOOS

PRACTICE MAKES PERFECT
T R D   M R K

Vault Editions Ltd

LEARN MORE

VAULTEDITIONS.COM

HOW TO DRAW
TATTOOS

PRACTICE
T R D MAKES M R K
PERFECT

PRACTICE
T R D MAKES M R K
PERFECT

Vault Editions Ltd

LEARN MORE

VAULTEDITIONS.COM

PRACTICE
MAKES
PERFECT
T R D
M R K

HOW TO DRAW
TATTOOS

PRACTICE
MAKES
PERFECT
T R D
M R K

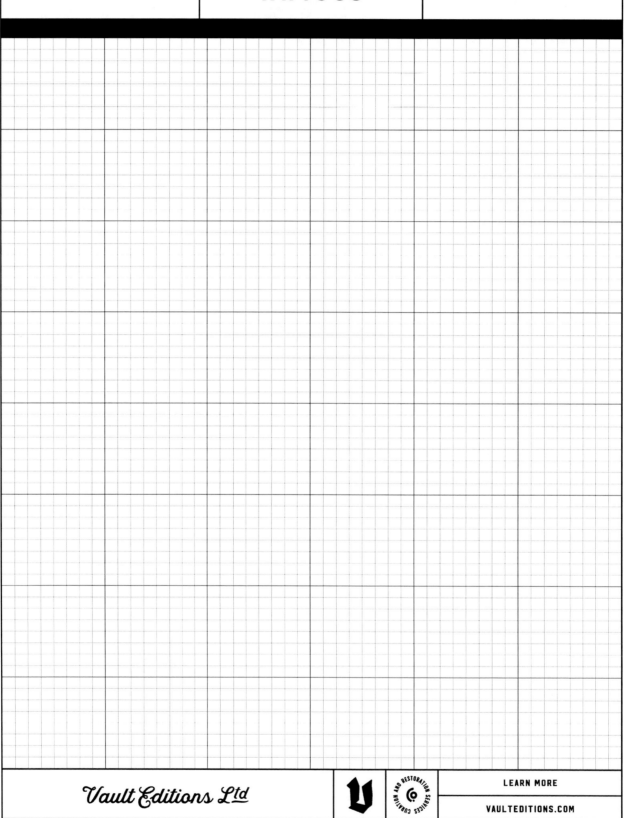

Vault Editions Ltd

LEARN MORE

VAULTEDITIONS.COM

CURATION AND RESTORATION SERVICES

HOW TO DRAW
TATTOOS

PRACTICE MAKES PERFECT
T R D MRK

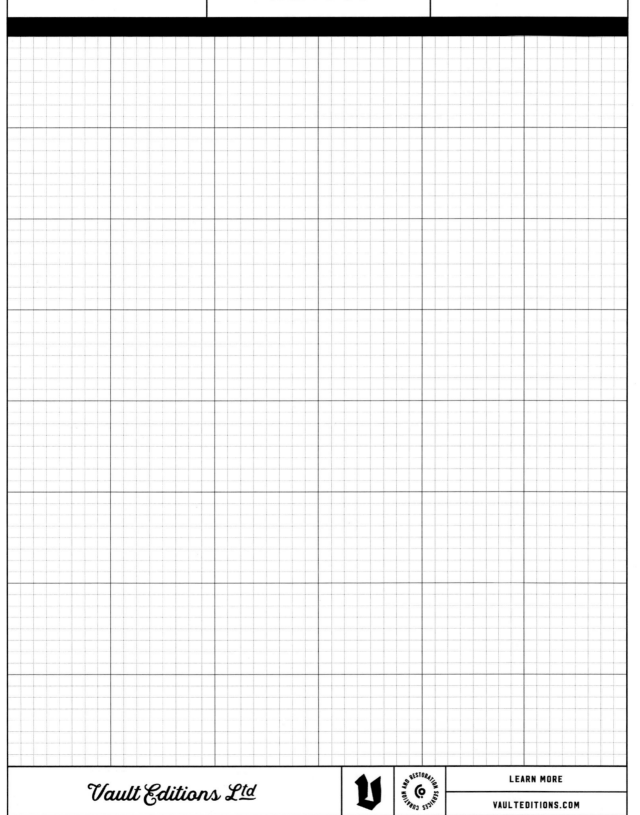

Vault Editions Ltd

CURATION AND RESTORATION SERVICES

LEARN MORE

VAULTEDITIONS.COM

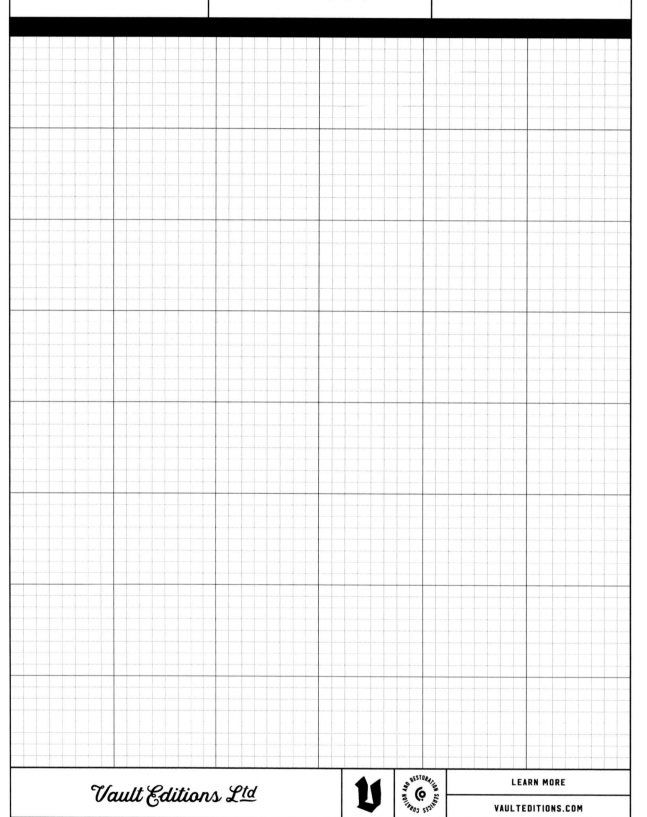

Vault Editions Ltd

LEARN MORE

VAULTEDITIONS.COM

PRACTICE MAKES PERFECT
T R D MRK

HOW TO DRAW
TATTOOS

PRACTICE MAKES PERFECT
T R D MRK

Vault Editions Ltd

LEARN MORE

VAULTEDITIONS.COM

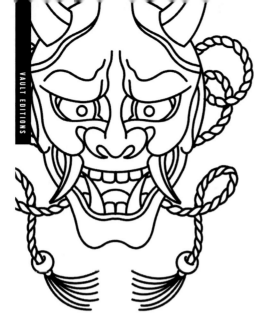

LEARN MORE

At Vault Editions, our mission is to create the world's most diverse and comprehensive collection of image archives available for artists, designers and curious minds. If you have enjoyed this book, you can find more of our titles available at vaulteditions.com.

REVIEW THIS BOOK

As a small, family-owned independent publisher, reviews help spread the word about our work. We would be incredibly grateful if you could leave an honest review of this title wherever you purchased this book.

JOIN OUR COMMUNITY

Are you a creative and curious individual? If so, you will love our community on Instagram. Every day we share bizarre and beautiful artwork ranging from 17th and 18th-century natural history and scientific illustration, to mythical beasts, ornamental designs, anatomical illustration and more. Join our community of 100K+ people today—search @vault_editions on Instagram.

DOWNLOAD YOUR FILES

STEP ONE

Enter the following web address in your web browser on a desktop computer.

www.vaulteditions.com/pages/htdt

STEP TWO

Enter the following unique password to access the download page.

htdt6472776348sxda

STEP THREE

Follow the prompts to access your high-resolution files.

TECHNICAL ASSISTANCE

For all technical assistance, please email: info@vaulteditions.com

Made in United States
North Haven, CT
04 May 2024

52131234R00062